Little-Known
FACTS
ABOUT
Well-Known
PLACES

DISNEYLAND

Little-Known FACTS ABOUT Well-Known PLACES

DISNEYLAND

DAVID HOFFMAN

FALL
RIVER
PRESS

Images: clipart.com

Fall River Press
122 Fifth Avenue
New York, NY 10011

ISBN: 978-1-4351-0431-0

Printed and bound in China

13 15 17 19 20 18 16 14

INTRODUCTION

Disneyland...a magic place of dreams and adventure. But for everything that we think we may know about the happiest place on earth, there is always a tidbit, a top secret, or a twist of fate that we have yet to discover.

Little-Known Facts about Well-Known Places goes beyond the obvious to reveal the stories behind the legend of this famous tourist destination that we all are familiar with—or at least think we're familiar with.

Covering every aspect of Disneyland—from the history and personalities to the landscaping and architecture—this collection of offbeat facts and figures, statistics and specifics, is guaranteed to delight a first-time visitor and surprise even the most die-hard fan.

Packed with a wealth of revelations that could start (or stop) a conversation—not to mention win a ton of bar bets—*Little-Known Facts about Well-Known Places* is a must-have for Mouseketeers, information addicts, curious readers, and armchair travelers of all ages.

Look for these other
titles in the series:

Little-Known
FACTS
ABOUT
Well-Known
PLACES

PARIS

ITALY

NEW YORK

IRELAND

The official address of Disneyland is 1313 Harbor Boulevard. Because there were no buildings (and hence no street addresses) in the neighborhood when the park was under construction, Walt was able to select the number. Some people believe that 13 stands for M, the thirteenth letter in the alphabet—thereby making the address "M.M.," for Mickey Mouse. But 1313 was also the number that Disney artists used as Donald Duck's address, and 313 was Donald's license plate number, so perhaps Walt simply liked "lucky" number 13.

When Disneyland opened its gates on July 17, 1955, it had just eighteen rides and attractions. Today there are more than sixty.

$1
cost of admission on opening day

28,154
park guests on opening day

13 MILLION
current number of annual park guests

Disney management still refers to opening day as "Black Sunday." Temperatures were unseasonably hot (well over 100 degrees), drinking fountains were dry (thanks to a plumbers' strike), toilets clogged, food ran out, there was a gas leak in Fantasyland, and women's high heels sank into the asphalt on Main Street. To make it easier for female guests to get around, they were given free pairs of moccasins, because those were the only shoes Disneyland sold for adults.

In 1955, Tomorrowland represented a city from 1986. That year was selected because it was the next scheduled appearance of Halley's Comet.

In addition to the likes of Tomorrowland, Fantasyland, and Adventureland, the park's original architectural plans included a Land of Oz. At the time, Walt Disney Studios owned the rights to L. Frank Baum's books.

In the park's planning stage, Tom Sawyer Island was called Mickey Mouse Island and was home to the Mickey Mouse Club and the Mouseketeers. Walt soon changed his mind, in part because Tom Sawyer made more sense for Frontierland, but mostly to insure, should the park go belly up, that Mickey would not be associated with the failure. This was also the reasoning behind the decision to have Tinkerbell, not Mickey, introduce the Disneyland TV series every week.

Disneyland's original Tinkerbell was Tiny Kline, a 4-foot-10-inch-tall circus performer and aerialist who was seventy-one years old when she first flew down a zipline from the top of the Matterhorn to start the "Fantasy in the Sky" fireworks show.

The "Remember… Dreams Come True" fireworks display created for Disneyland's 50th anniversary was the most elaborate ever put on at the park, and its development was so top secret that designers went all the way to China's Gobi Desert to do the trial run.

$41,000

cost, per night, of the
fireworks show above
Sleeping Beauty Castle

100,000

light bulbs outlining the buildings
on Main Street

54

full-time electricians employed
by Disneyland

eople who work at Disneyland are not referred to as employees; rather, they are called "cast members." Cast members who don a character costume and walk around the park greeting guests refer to that as having "duck duty." They also call It's a Small World "the asylum," on the theory that that's where they'll end up as a result of repeated (over)exposure to the ride's theme song.

The toughest part about doing "duck duty" is wearing the costume. On average, a character costume weighs forty pounds, and during the hot summer months, under the blazing sun and surrounded by crowds, the inside can heat up to 150 degrees.

Initially, all cast members doing "duck duty" could talk to park guests, but in the early 1970s, management ruled that "voice clearance was reserved for face characters"; today, only those characters (like Snow White, Jack Sparrow or Alice in Wonderland) whose actual faces are visible are allowed to speak.

Being a character is one of the most gratifying jobs in the park, but all that adoration from hoards of guests can be dangerous. While villains, such as Captain Hook, do get booed or kicked, the most vulnerable costumes are the Seven Dwarfs and the Three Little Pigs, because they are among the smallest.

New cast members are sent to Disney University and go through a three- to five-day training course called "Traditions," where they learn that Disneyland is not the normal workplace. It is a stage— and their job is putting on a show.

First names are featured on the name badges worn by all Disneyland (and Disney) employees, regardless of their position within the company. This practice dates back to 1962 and Walt's dislike of being called "Mr. Disney." Prior to this, Disney employee ID tags simply identified cast members with numbers.

One of the employees of Disneyland in the 1960s was Steve Martin, who honed his talent for crafting balloon animals—a staple of his early standup act—while working at the Magic Shop. Other famous former cast members include Michelle Pfeiffer (who played Alice in Wonderland in the Main Street Electrical Parade), actress Rene Russo, and Ron Ziegler (press secretary to Richard Nixon, who did duty as a skipper on the Jungle Cruise).

Former Secretary of State Henry Kissinger was such a fan of Disneyland that in the 1970s he would visit to get lost in the crowd and escape from the stress and pressure of his job. One day, for fun, he put on a uniform and sold popcorn from a cart. People gave him a second look, especially on hearing his distinctive voice and accent, but he still went the whole shift unrecognized.

One fail-proof way to identify your location in the park: check out the garbage cans. While uniform in size and shape, they are painted a different color in each of the different "lands."

The ground at the entrance to the park is red to simulate a red carpet, and to make every guest feel like a V.I.P.; on entering Main Street, the pavement becomes black, because black gets hot and "hot" keeps crowds moving—not just into the park, but directly into Main Street shops.

There is no elaborate system of tunnels connecting all of Disneyland underground; still, the park does have some interesting subterranean spaces, including one narrow walkway that runs below Tomorrowland (from beneath Innoventions to the area opposite the southern end of the Matterhorn). While it is occasionally used to get performers to and from the Club Buzz stage, its primary purpose is for trash removal and maintenance.

500

toy brooms used annually to keep Disneyland clean

30

tons of garbage Disneyland generates in one day

1,850

tons of garbage Disneyland recycles yearly

isneyland's New Orleans Square is several stories high, and as a result, the boarding area for Pirates of the Caribbean is on the equivalent of the third floor. What's underneath? The lower level of the attraction, along with offices, the main kitchen for this part of the park, and "the DEC" (the Disney Employee Caféteria). The entrance to this area can be found to the immediate left of the Disneyland Railroad's New Orleans Square station, just before the restrooms.

Disneyland may be a world unto itself, but technically it is part of the city of Anaheim, so park construction must adhere to municipal building codes. This can get interesting: special considerations had to be made for the Matterhorn because, at 147 feet, it exceeded the city's maximum height allowances; and local ordinances had to be amended for Submarine Voyage, given that land-locked Anaheim had no provisions on the books pertaining to the operation of underwater vessels within city limits.

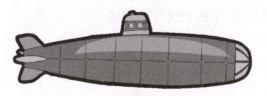

The opening of Submarine Voyage in 1959, followed by the Matterhorn and the Monorail, inaugurated the E ticket. Up until that time, there had only been A, B, C, and D tickets. The last E-ticket ride added to Disneyland before the park switched to the current "passport system" was Big Thunder Mountain Railroad, in 1979.

Since November 2005, it has become a tradition that the turkey "pardoned" by the president of the United States on Thanksgiving Day is sent to Disneyland to live on the grounds of Big Thunder Ranch.

The topography surrounding Big Thunder Mountain Railroad was based on the tall, thin spires of rock found in abundance at Bryce Canyon National Park in Utah.

isneyland's Matterhorn was the first roller coaster to use tubular steel instead of wood for its track; and therefore it was the first to allow loops, corkscrews, and extreme changes in direction.

The Matterhorn has two different tracks, and which one you ride is determined by which of the two lines you choose to wait in. Seasoned park-goers know that the right line (next to Alice in Wonderland, in Fantasyland) puts you on the slower track, where the ride lasts 30 seconds longer, while the left line (towards Tomorrowland) feeds into the faster track, which has one unexpected drop and tighter turns.

There is a regulation-size half-court on which employees can play basketball inside the Matterhorn.

Disneyland's Matterhorn is a 1:100 scale replica of the real mountain located in the Swiss Alps.

Sleeping Beauty Castle rises only seventy-two feet above the moat (making it no larger than an average four-story building). To create the illusion of size, designers employed "forced perspective," a trick in which things are scaled smaller as they are built higher—thus making structures appear bigger, taller, and grander than they actually are. The same construction technique was used on the storefronts on Main Street, where from the ground floor to the third story, the scale shifts from 9/10ths to 7/8ths to 5/8ths actual size.

The inspiration for Sleeping Beauty Castle came from Neuschwanstein Castle in Bavaria, Germany, which was built by Ludwig II in homage to opera composer Richard Wagner.

Prior to 2001, guests could walk through Sleeping Beauty Castle (it was lined with windows housing dioramas based on the animated film). Its closure in 2001 was not only because it was not ADA-compliant (due to narrow corridors and winding staircases), but was also a result of post 9/11 terrorist fears.

The story that one spire of Sleeping Beauty Castle remains purposely unplated to visually represent Walt's theory that "Disneyland will never be completed as long as there is imagination left in the world" makes good copy, but it's not true. Rather, when the castle was refurbished in the 1990s, that spire was finished with a patina process that was expected to yield better results than the gold leafing previously used. It didn't—and ultimately, the ensuing dullness simply made the spire look like it had been forgotten.

The coat of arms hanging directly over the drawbridge entrance to Sleeping Beauty Castle is the Disney family crest.

The drawbridge to Sleeping Beauty Castle is not just there for show; still, in the park's history, it has only been raised and lowered twice—during the televised grand opening of Disneyland and at the 1983 rededication of the new and improved Fantasyland.

The vegetation that lines the moat around Sleeping Beauty Castle primarily consists of junipers because it is one of the few types of foliage that swans will not eat.

The swans in the moat around Sleeping Beauty Castle are leased by the park, and there is always one male and one female.

There is a sizeable colony of feral cats in and around Disneyland, although park-goers do not usually see them due to their nocturnal nature. The grounds crews leave them alone, primarily because (and how ironic is this?) they help to keep the rodent population in check.

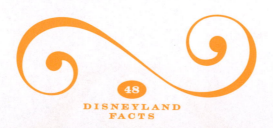

Walt was afraid of mice.

The all-time most popular Disneyland souvenir is a pair of personalized Mickey Mouse ears. While the embroidery is free, the Mad Hatter and other shops that sell them will not allow guests to have them adorned with the name of a famous person, corporation, sports team or personal business. This does not stop guests from getting creative; one requested that "Vincent" be written on his, then after it was handed back to him, he tore off one of the ears.

78 MILLION

pairs of Mickey Mouse ears purchased between opening day and Disneyland's 50th anniversary in 2005 (enough to adorn every child in America under 18)

80

different styles of postcards in Disney souvenir shops that feature an image of Sleeping Beauty Castle

1760110

Registered Trademark No. for "the configuration of a round head with round mouse ears attached"

In designing, constructing, adding the final touches to, or upgrading an attraction, Disney artists often pay homage to the Mouse by subtly incorporating a silhouette of Mickey into the design. (Most commonly, the silhouette consists of three circles to represent his round head and two round ears.) Die-hard Disney fans make a game of searching for these "Hidden Mickeys" throughout the park—there are dozens to be found.

One of the first Hidden Mickeys was the model of the giant water molecule in the old Adventure Thru Inner Space attraction, where two small hydrogen atoms were positioned atop a single larger oxygen atom, forming not only H_2O, but a representation of the familiar Mickey face.

Adventure Thru Inner Space, the popular Tomorrowland attraction which (from 1967 to 1985) took passengers on a journey into the depths of an atom, was so dark inside that amorous park-goers took to using it as a place to get intimate—and cast members took to calling it "Adventure Thru Intercourse."

Despite the security systems now installed inside all of Disneyland's attractions (and the monitors being watched by park employees hidden from view), couples will still try to have sex while on the "dark" rides (such as Pirates of the Caribbean or It's a Small World), apparently not realizing that the cameras are infrared and can pick up their every move. On occasion they are stopped with a warning over the loudspeaker; other times, as they exit, they are met with applause from knowing cast members.

Although the majority of the officers are dressed in plain clothes and go unnoticed, Disneyland's security force has more members than the City of Anaheim has police.

For years, individual shops, vendors, and restaurants in Disneyland would accept just about any foreign currency, provided that the United States kept diplomatic relations with that country. Today, the currency must be exchanged first at City Hall.

The least crowded time to visit Disneyland is the period following Thanksgiving weekend and leading up to Christmas.

Studies show that during prime meal hours, when the self-serve food operations are at their busiest, the lines on the left side tend to be shorter.

o avoid the lines at any popular attraction that does not offer a Fastpass, instead of heading there first, save it for last. It is park practice that unless an attraction plans to shut down early (cast members on the attraction will know if this is the case), anyone in line at the time of closing will be able to remain in line until they are able to board and ride.

One of the best in-park views of the fireworks display—from the second-floor platform of the Main Street train station—also puts guests in a position for the quickest exit.

The musical soundtrack cannot be heard, but the Disneyland fireworks show can easily be watched from outside the park. A primo spot with an unobstructed view (and it's free!) is the small area at the northeast corner of the intersection of West Ball Road and South Anaheim Boulevard, by the entrance to the Sheraton hotel and across the street from the cast members' parking lot.

Many days at Disneyland begin with a "rope drop" that lets everyone in at once. The rope is positioned at the northern end of Main Street, where the shopping district ends. However, if your first stop is either Fantasyland or Tomorrowland, instead of gathering there with the masses, consider slipping into one of the already opened shops on the east side of the street. Work your way through the shops—they're all connected—until you reach the side exit in the far back. This will not only put you even with the front of the Main Street crowd, but (once the ropes drop) a valuable few steps ahead of them.

Anyone, not just cast members, can wake up José the Macaw in the Enchanted Tiki Room. Simply ask a cast member as you enter, while the audience is being seated.

Among the other things at Disneyland that are yours (or your kids') for the asking: a seat at the front of the Monorail and a ride in the wheelhouse of the Mark Twain Riverboat.

Besides alcohol, the only food or drink banned from sale inside Disneyland is gum. Walt did not want his guests to constantly be stepping in it or picking it off their shoes, a pet peeve he had with other amusement parks.

The most popular food item at Disneyland is ice cream. Main Street's Gibson Girl Parlor alone sells enough yearly to build a life-size replica of the Matterhorn.

In the mid-1950s and continuing through the 1960s, animation cels, which can now command four and five figures, were considered fun to look at, but worthless, so thousands of original scenes from Disney movies were sold at the park as souvenirs—for a buck each.

City Hall not only supplies maps and guides to Disneyland, it provides them in five other languages (Chinese, Japanese, French, Spanish, and German) besides English.

The idea of Main Street was inspired by Walt's childhood hometown of Marceline, Missouri, but chief designer Harper Goff had grown up in Fort Collins, Colorado, so much of the architectural style is based on that city— in particular City Hall, which was modeled after the Fort Collins County Courthouse.

Tom Sawyer Island was officially annexed and recognized by the Missouri State Legislature in 1956.

The water tower adjacent to Frontierland is active and fully functional—and it is the source of power for the steam trains on the Disneyland Railroad.

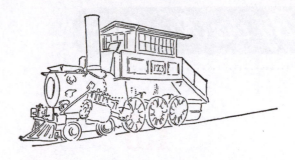

The four original locomotives on the Disneyland Railroad were named after four executives of the Santa Fe Railroad: C.K. Holiday, E.P. Ripley, Ernest S. Marsh, and Fred Gurley. Walt, a train buff, always had a soft spot for the Santa Fe, as it ran through his Missouri hometown.

1.5
length, in miles, of the
Disneyland Railroad

20,000
miles per year that the train on
the Disneyland Railroad travels
(just by circling the park)

20
minutes it takes to ride the
Disneyland Railroad around
the perimeter of the park

The Grand Canyon diorama, visible only from the Disneyland Railroad as it travels between Tomorrowland and Main Street, measures 306 feet and is the longest diorama in the world.

Among the items that have turned up in the Disneyland lost and found: false teeth, a prosthetic limb, a glass eye, toupees, a waterbed, and a canary.

The Town Square flagpole is recycled from a lamppost that once stood on Wilshire Boulevard in Los Angeles, and was purchased from the city for five dollars, after the fixture was knocked over in a car accident.

DISNEYLAND FACTS

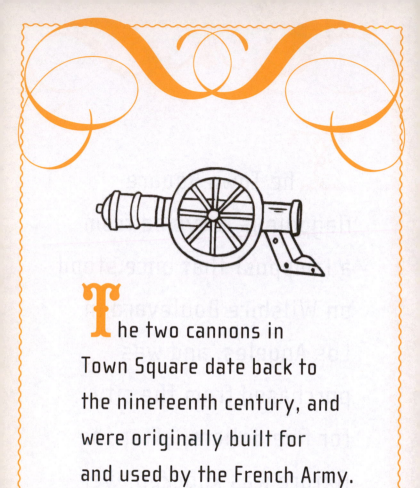

The two cannons in Town Square date back to the nineteenth century, and were originally built for and used by the French Army.

The gas streetlamps on Main Street are over 150 years old and were bought as scrap, for as little as three cents a pound, from St. Louis, Baltimore, and Philadephia, which had no further use for them. It proved to be a good deal on several levels: in December 1982, the park had to be evacuated due to a power outage, and the gas lamps lit the way.

Each light in Disneyland is replaced when it has reached 80 percent of its design life rather than when it fails.

There are no sharp 90-degree angles in the Main Street sidewalks. Walt felt that they would give the park a certain urban coldness, so to guarantee that Disneyland maintained its small town sense of warmth, all of the curbs were constructed using curves instead of corners.

For the first year Disneyland was in operation, the Main Street Penny Arcade included a shooting gallery that used real guns—live ammunition .22-caliber rifles.

Among the original stores on Main Street—between the Silhouette Shop and the China Closet—was the Hollywood Maxwell Corset Shop, also known as "The Wizard of Bras."

To encourage guests to buy sweatshirts and warm clothing, the Disney Clothiers, Ltd. store is kept several degrees cooler than the other shops on Main Street.

Though not open to the public, there is a 600-square-foot apartment over the Main Street Fire Station, where Walt would occasionally stay when he visited the park. It is used today by visiting executives, the Disney family, and for small, private meetings.

The names painted on the second-story windows along Main Street are those of people who played a key role in Disneyland, the Walt Disney Company, or Disney's life. This was Walt's way of thanking, and permanently honoring, those who helped him realize his vision.

Names of Disneylanders who created, and continued to develop, the park's attractions can be found painted on the signs, buildings, boxes, trunks, and barrels incorporated into the design of various rides and lands, from the tombstones at the Haunted Mansion to the stacks of crates next to the Jungle Cruise.

"**B**enjamin Silverstein, M.D.," the name that appears on the Main Street door with a mezuzah next to it, was not a real person; rather, the façade was created so that there would be a fitting place for the park to put up Hanukkah decorations.

hough no longer marked by signs, the two roads that intersect the east side of Main Street also have names: Center Street and Plaza Street.

The Disneyland Band was to play for a two-week engagement when the park first opened, but proved so popular that it has been "held over" for fifty years.

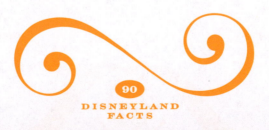

The tiny pieces embedded into the pavement of Main Street (often mistaken for discarded chewing gum) are sensors that guide parade floats and ensure they hit their marks.

The tracks running down Main Street are greased each morning with vegetable oil, so that the streetcars can round corners safely, efficiently, and quietly.

The horses pulling streetcars on Main Street have a polyurethane coating on their shoes, partially because it gives them better traction, but mainly to heighten the clip-clop sound they make as they walk.

The depiction of Walt in the bronze "Partners" statue at the end of Main Street shows him wearing a tiepin with a stylized "STR" logo—the emblem for Smoke Tree Ranch in Palm Springs, California, a favorite vacation destination of his.

Designers modeling the Audio-Animatronic Abe to be used in Great Moments with Mr. Lincoln inadvertently discovered that when the rubber mold of the head was turned inside out, the President's eyes would appear to follow them wherever they went. The effect was creepy...so creepy that they incorporated this technique into the Haunted Mansion and cast the two busts found at the end of the hallway (as you exit the elevator) from molds that had been deliberately inverted.

The dancing ghosts in the ballroom of the Haunted Mansion are created through the use of an old magician's trick: the actual robots and mannequins going through the motions are concealed one story above, but are lit in a way that their ghostly likenesses are reflected in the glass in front of you.

The PeopleMover track system used to transport guests in the Haunted Mansion without relying on wheeled carriages was inspired by a conveyor belt (which was designed to safely lift and transport hot metal ingots) that Walt had seen on a visit to the Ford Motor Company plant.

The hardest task facing the maintenance crew assigned to the Haunted Mansion is keeping it looking dirty enough, so they regularly haul in cobwebs and five-pound bags of dust, which they then scatter around with a device similar to a fertilizer spreader.

The voice and face of the fallen bust in the Haunted Mansion belongs to Thurl Ravenscroft, who is not only the narrator of the Disneyland Railroad, but was (until his death in 2005) the voice of Tony the Tiger.

The most unusual Disneyland souvenir ever offered by the park was the opportunity to have a personalized tombstone placed in the graveyard at the Haunted Mansion. It sold at auction for $37,400; the proceeds went to charity.

To give the grounds outside the Haunted Mansion a sense of decay, particular varieties of heucheras, ipomeas, and ajungas were selected by the landscape architects for their washed-out brown and dark green hues. If they were simply replaced with red, purple, and pink varieties of the same plants, the gardens would then be beautiful.

45,000
trees and shrubs planted in
Disneyland each year

1 MILLION
annuals planted yearly in Disneyland

150
landscape gardeners employed
by Disneyland

10,000
flowers it takes to complete
the Mickey Mouse portrait at the
entrance to the park

To create the Mickey Mouse floral portrait at the park entrance, gardeners install fiberglass header board into the soil to form the ears, eyes, nose, mouth, and cheeks. They then plant annuals of designated colors into each segment, much like painting by numbers.

Many of the plants in and around Tomorrowland are edible, to emphasize a future where gardens do double duty as food sources. This is most noticeable in the bushes along the walkways, which are planted with lettuce, kale, rhubarb, and an assortment of herbs.

Hedges throughout the park are treated with growth-retarding hormones to limit the need for pruning. Olive trees are also sprayed, to prevent their fruit from maturing and falling, making it easier for maintenance crews to keep the sidewalks clean.

The names of virtually every plant and tree in the park are kept on file at City Hall. The  records are open to any guest interested in knowing more about any of the landscaping they have seen.

While Tarzan's Treehouse (formerly the Swiss Family Robinson Treehouse) has been given the species name Disneyodendron, it was modeled after a real tree—a Moreton Bay Fig—that still stands less than two miles north of the park, in front of the house at 410 N. West Street in Anaheim.

150 TONS

weight of the "tree" that holds Tarzan's Treehouse

6,000

leaves, all applied by hand, on the tree that holds Tarzan's Treehouse

42 FEET

depth of the roots of the tree that holds Tarzan's Treehouse

4

treehouses in Disneyland: Tarzan's, Chip 'n Dale's, Tom and Huck's, and the "Treehouse of Technology" at Innoventions in Tomorrowland

Building Disneyland used up all of Walt's capital, so in a quest to find a way to develop and test his latest ideas but with someone else footing the bill, it hit him to contact major corporations and offer to create attractions for them for the 1964 World's Fair. Among his clients were General Motors, General Electric, Ford, and Pepsi-Cola, and among the results was It's A Small World.

The gold decorating the exterior of It's A Small World isn't paint but, in fact, 22-karat gold leaf. And not just because it looks amazing; gold leaf is, over time, more cost-effective, since it does not need to be replaced as often.

A journey through It's a Small World passes by children of over a hundred different nationalities and takes guests through dozens of different countries; however, the United States is not depicted. Similarly, while the United States is represented in the overseas parks, you will not find Japan in Tokyo Disneyland or France at Disneyland Paris.

According to the International Museum of Carousel Art, there is no difference between a carousel and a merry-go-round. While it is common that one-third of the animals on both are stationary, what sets Disneyland's King Arthur's Carousel apart is that it has been modified so that not only do all of the animals move, but all of the animals are horses and all of the horses are jumpers.

In the beginning, only one of the horses on King Arthur's Carousel was white. It proved so popular that all of the horses are now white, yet all are painted differently.

A lesser-known spot from which to watch the nightly fireworks display is by the planters that surround King Arthur's Carousel. Not only does the edge of the planter provide a rare place to sit, but Tinkerbell's flight path takes her directly over you.

In Peter Pan's Flight, as pirate ships escort park visitors through the window of the Darling children's bedroom, over London, and on to Neverland, observant guests will notice a set of blocks, whose letters spell out D-I-S-N-E-Y from the bottom up.

While experimenting with methods to make the miniature church roof in the Storybook Land Canal Boat Ride appear realistically old and weathered, a designer discovered that urine has an extremely corrosive effect on metal. So...

The Dumbo ride was first conceived as "Pink Elephants on Parade" and was to consist of all pink elephants, like the ones that Dumbo envisions in his nightmare in the movie. Walt changed his mind, however, when he realized that it might look like he was encouraging kids to drink alcohol.

When President Harry Truman—a Democrat—visited Disneyland in 1957, he refused to ride on Dumbo, as he did not wish to be photographed with a giant elephant, the symbol of the Republican Party.

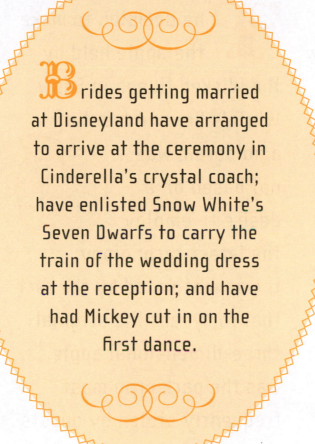

Brides getting married at Disneyland have arranged to arrive at the ceremony in Cinderella's crystal coach; have enlisted Snow White's Seven Dwarfs to carry the train of the wedding dress at the reception; and have had Mickey cut in on the first dance.

The decision to make the apple held by the Wicked Queen in Snow White's Scary Adventure a hologram was not based on a desire to employ the latest technology; it was motivated by the fact that for years the original three-dimensional apple was the park prop most frequently stolen by guests seeking souvenirs.

Initially, the storybook rides were designed so that guests could experience the attraction from the main character's point of view—so guests on Snow White's Scary Adventure WERE Snow White. But for years, nobody got it, and guests would regularly ask cast members where Snow White—or Peter Pan or Alice in Wonderland—was. This was the main reason that Fantasyland was completely overhauled in 1983, and why today namesake characters are featured in their own rides.

The tag marked "10/6" that pokes out of the Mad Hatter's hat is a price tag, indicating the cost of the hat to be ten shillings, sixpence.

Of the eighteen teacups available to ride on the Mad Tea Party, the plain lavender one spins the fastest.

To make the teacups on the Mad Tea Party spin faster:

✦ The weight of all passengers should be evenly distributed.

✦ All riders should lean toward the center.

✦ Riders should take turns spinning the wheel—if more than two people do it, hands get in each other's way, and can slow you down.

The attraction most responsible for causing park guests to lose their lunch is the Mad Tea Party. To clean up the mess, a cast member covers it with "Barf Dust," a green, kitty litter-like substance that soaks up the mishap and enables it to be swept up easily.

Walt had the idea for Space Mountain in the 1960s but the technology was not available for its creation until a decade later.

Space Mountain had to be sunk nearly 20 feet into the ground when it was built so that it would be in proper proportion to Sleeping Beauty Castle and the Matterhorn.

The soundtrack you hear while riding Space Mountain is performed by Dick Dale, "King of the Surf Guitar."

Even at its
fastest, Space
Mountain never
goes more than
30.3 miles per hour.

R2-D2 and C-3PO, seen in the waiting area at Star Tours, are props from the original *Star Wars* film. The overlay on C-3PO is real gold; it was the only substance that gave off the shine that director George Lucas wanted, and the only coating guaranteed not to rust during production.

The announcement that plays in the waiting area leading into Star Tours twice pays tribute to *Star Wars* director George Lucas: first, there is the page for "departing passenger Sacul... Mr. Egroeg Sacul..." ("Egroeg Sacul" is George Lucas spelled backwards); later, it is broadcast that a "landspeeder with the license plate THX1138 is parked in a no-hover zone." (*THX1138* was Lucas's first film).

Disneyland has numerous attractions based on movies, and numerous movies have been based on Disneyland attractions, yet in all these years, only two movies have ever been filmed on location at the park: *Forty Pounds of Trouble* (with Tony Curtis and Suzanne Pleshette) and Tom Hanks' *That Thing You Do*.

Captain EO, the 1986 3-D film attraction that starred Michael Jackson and Angelica Huston and was directed by Francis Ford Coppola, ran seventeen minutes and cost $17 million to produce, making it, at that time, minute for minute, the most expensive motion picture ever made—a record it held until *Titanic* was released eleven years later.

DISNEYLAND FACTS

The voice of Rex (officially, his name is RX-24), the bumbling android captain who takes guests on Star Tours, is that of actor Paul Reubens, better known as Pee-Wee Herman.

In the mid-1960s, when the novelty of Submarine Voyage started to diminish, Disneyland executives attempted to revitalize it by stocking the lagoon with live "mermaids" in bikini tops. The gimmick didn't last long, and it had unexpected consequences: young male guests took to jumping into the lagoon and swimming out to have their photos taken with the maidens, and several of the performers became ill from the chemicals in the water.

Submarine Voyage was comprised of eight vessels, which inadvertently made Walt the commander of the world's eighth-largest submarine fleet— a fact that caught the attention of then-Soviet Premier Nikita Khrushchev. Ultimately, Khrushchev's trip to Disneyland to see them was canceled by the U.S. State Department, over concerns that security was not adequate.

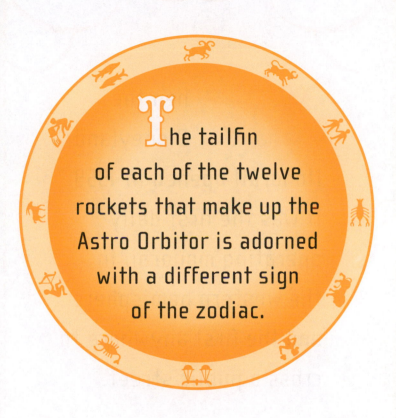

The tailfin
of each of the twelve
rockets that make up the
Astro Orbitor is adorned
with a different sign
of the zodiac.

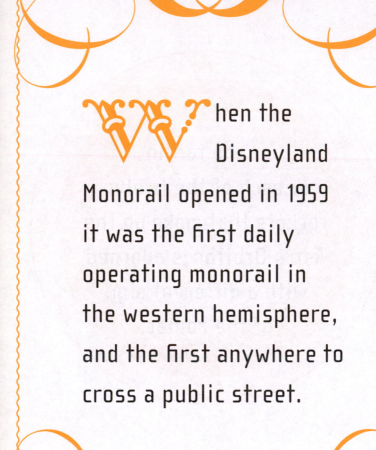

When the Disneyland Monorail opened in 1959 it was the first daily operating monorail in the western hemisphere, and the first anywhere to cross a public street.

The first passengers to officially ride the Monorail were then-Vice President Richard Nixon and his family. This also marked—unbeknownst to Nixon, the Secret Service, and the press—the first time that the futuristic vehicle had made it all the way around the park without incident. In the days (hours!) leading up to the ribbon-cutting ceremony, every time the engineers had sent the Monorail around its track for a test run, it had caught fire.

By the Numbers

110,000
passengers the Monorail carries
on an average day

99.9 PERCENT
"on time" rate of Monorail

20 MINUTES
minimum time it takes to restart
a ride due to computer and
safety protocols

160,000
different ride combinations that
guests can experience on the
Indiana Jones Adventure

The transports used in the Indiana Jones Adventure do not travel at greater speeds than the vehicles on other attractions in the park; rather, thanks to a motion simulator that is part of their base, they just feel like they do. As a result, guests get the impression that they are moving 65 mph, when in reality they are never going faster than 22 mph.

While most Audio-Animatronics of humans are mechanical forms that are ultimately, like mannequins, dressed in costume, the Indiana Jones figure was molded fully clothed, entirely out of rubber. Apparently, Audio-Animatronics are prone to leaking. The appeal of rubber, versus a traditional cloth wardrobe that would need to be removed, washed, laundered, pressed, and replaced, is that it can be cleaned with a simple scrubbing.

When designer Harriet Burns was looking for the perfect material to use to make the "skin" for the birds in the Enchanted Tiki Room, she had to look no further than her boss: in a meeting, she noticed that the cashmere sweater Walt was wearing moved at the elbows exactly the way that she needed.

The Enchanted Tiki Room is the only attraction in the park with its own restrooms. This is because it was initially planned as a restaurant with a dinner show, but the Audio-Animatronic part turned out to be so spectacular and well-received that the dining concept was scrapped before opening.

According to early drawings, Adventureland was on the east side of the park, next to Tomorrowland. The location was changed when it was discovered that there was a pre-exisiting grove of eucalyptus trees on the west side of the property, which designers felt would work well with the exotic Polynesian motif that they were planning.

Walt's original park plan incorporated using a number of the orange trees on the property, so he tagged the ones he wanted to stay with red ribbons and marked the ones he wanted removed with green ribbons. Unfortunately, the bulldozer operator was color-blind, so, after he was done, none of the trees were left standing.

By the Numbers

160

acres of former orange groves on
which Disneyland was built

365

days it took to complete construction
of Disneyland

$17 MILLION

cost, including the land, to build
Disneyland in 1954

$17 MILLION

cost to construct Splash Mountain
in 1989

Splash Mountain has earned the nickname "Flash Mountain" thanks to those uninhibited female park-goers who have taken to lifting up their tops and exposing their breasts to the cameras snapping souvenir photos at the final waterfall. While any off-color images are supposed to be deleted by Disneyland employees, they often get saved, and many are now circulating on the Internet. Unzip-a-dee-doo-dah!

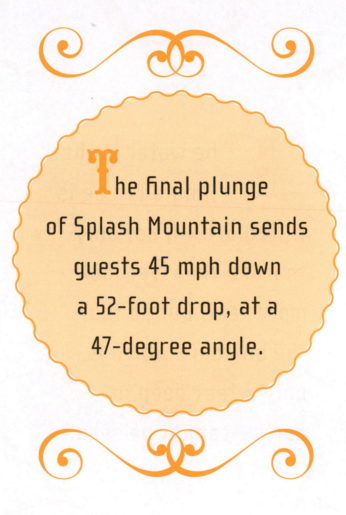

The final plunge of Splash Mountain sends guests 45 mph down a 52-foot drop, at a 47-degree angle.

The water in the Jungle Cruise is tinted brown, not only to make the river look more real, but so that the bottom—which is only 3 feet deep in parts—cannot be seen.

When the Jungle Cruise opened it was based on *True Life Adventures*, Disney's popular series of nature documentaries, and was designed as a realistic journey through the rivers of Asia, Africa, and South America. From the start, the tour was narrated by a skipper, but his original spiel was, in the spirit of the films, fact-filled and straight-forward. The current version—and its plethora of bad puns—did not follow until some years later, when more comic elements were incorporated into the ride.

Walt's initial plan for the Jungle Cruise was that it would be inhabited by real hippos and elephants until the practicality of working with live animals—particularly in such a tiny area—caught up with him. Beyond the worry that wildlife, afraid of humans, might spend the day hiding or sleeping and out of sight of the guests came the realization that animals need to be fed, and animals who eat tend to leave a trail behind them.

The revolvers fired by the skippers during the Jungle Cruise are bona fide nickel-plated Smith & Wesson .38 Specials, which have been altered so that live ammo cannot be used in them.

The blank ammo utilized on the Jungle Cruise comes in two forms, each of which makes a different sound when fired. "Show ammo," quieter and more commonly heard, is used to scare the hippos from attacking the boat; "Breakdown ammo" is what the skippers use in case of emergency to signal the foreman back at the dock that there has been a problem (three shots indicate mechanical difficulties; four shots signify a medical or security emergency).

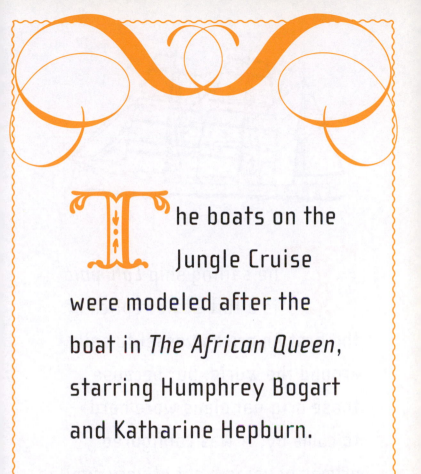

The boats on the Jungle Cruise were modeled after the boat in *The African Queen*, starring Humphrey Bogart and Katharine Hepburn.

The sailing ship *Columbia* is a full-scale replica of the first American vessel to sail around the world, but because those original plans were hard to come by, it was configured primarily using a set of very similar plans—those of the HMS *Bounty* of *Mutiny on the Bounty* fame.

The Mark Twain Riverboat is a genuine paddle wheeler, yet while it runs on steam, it does so without needing a captain to navigate it—thanks to a carefully hidden, underwater guidance track.

7

horsepower generated by
an Autopia car

4.4 MPH

speed of the horses on
King Arthur's Carousel

1/3 MILE

length of the one-way trip,
via horse-drawn streetcar,
down Main Street

9

minutes it takes to ride the
Monorail from start to finish

The underground, inter-terminal train that has been operating at George Bush Intercontinental Airport in Houston since 1981 replicates the exact mechanical design of the Tomorrowland PeopleMover and is the only transportation system outside of a Disney park that was built by the Walt Disney Company.

The passport sitting in the glass case along the back wall of Mickey's house in Toontown is stamped with the names of five places (Anaheim, Orlando, Hong Kong, Paris, and Tokyo), each a city where a Disney park is located. The date of the stamp is the same as the date that the property officially opened.

Among the books lining the shelves of Minnie's house is one in the kitchen that's entitled, "Elvis. What Happened?"

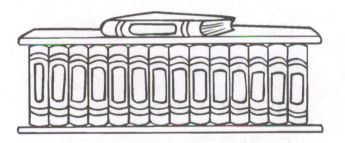

Wayne Allwine, the actor who has provided the voice for Mickey Mouse for the last twenty-five years, and Russi Taylor, who has done Minnie's voice for about the same amount of time, are husband and wife in real life. They met on the job.

Though certainly well-known, Mickey Mouse is not the most recognizable character in the world; he ranks third, after Santa Claus and Ronald McDonald.

He's Mickey Mouse to you and me, but in Iran, he's known as Mickey Moosh; in Iceland, Mikki Mus; in Italy, Topolino; and in Sweden, Musse Pigg.

Donald Duck's nephews—Huey, Dewey, and Louie—were named after Louisiana politician Huey Long, New York politician Thomas Dewey, and Disney animator Louis Schmitt.

The locked blue-green doorway on Royal Street in New Orleans Square, with the ornate address plate bearing the number 33, is not just another fun design detail, but marks the entrance to a private dining room known as Club 33. Inspired by the numerous companies who offered restricted access lounges to VIPs visiting their pavilions at the 1964 World's Fair, Walt wanted a place in Disneyland where he could entertain investors and business associates. It's also the only place in the park that serves alcohol.

Membership in Club 33 currently stands at about 487 individuals and corporations. The limit is due to the capacity of the restaurant, more than snobbery or exclusivity.

Club 33 has a nine-year waiting list (at times, it's been as long as fourteen years) that caps at 1,000 people. It, too, is totally full.

In 2007, corporations were paying $25,000 to join Club 33, plus $5,925 in annual dues. For individuals, it was $9,500 initially, and $3,175 annually.

In the planning stages, the smaller of the two Club 33 dining areas was to have microphones hidden in the overhead chandeliers. It is rumored that this set-up was Richard Nixon's idea, so that Walt could eavesdrop on guests. Not true. The primary reason for using listening devices was to allow actors to entertain the members by conversing with them in the guise of the Audio-Animatronic critters perched throughout the room. However, while all of these features were installed (hidden microphones and one Turkey Vulture are still visible amid the club's decor), they were never activated.

It has often been reported that Club 33 got its numerical name from its address, and that the address itself was required in order for Disneyland to get a liquor license, but this theory is unlikely since neither streets nor addresses inside the park are recognized by the United States Postal Service.

There are several theories about why the club was named Club 33. Among them:

- ✦ The number '33' turned sideways, reads M.M. (for Mickey Mouse) and looks like mouse ears.

- ✦ When Walt passed away months prior to the club's completion, the future of the club was in jeopardy. Of the forty-seven park investors consulted about the future of the club, thirty-three voted to continue with the construction, keeping Walt's vision alive.

- ✦ The number 33 represents the number of original park sponsors and lessees.

- ✦ Club 33 is the only place in the park that sells alcohol and 1933 was the year that prohibition was repealed.

The tapping sound coming from the Depot at the Disneyland Railroad station in New Orleans Square is a line from Walt's opening day speech ("To all who come to this happy place, welcome...") in a variant of Morse code. However, early on in the park's history, the designers varied the messages, and often, for fun, they would make them off-color comments—until Walt happened to mention that his wife Lillian had been a telegraph operator and could decipher Morse code.

All of the railings surrounding the second-floor balconies of New Orleans Square that are visible to guests, yet not accessible to them, are made of rubber instead of cast iron, as rubber will not rust and stands a better chance of weathering the elements.

The huge box office success of *Mary Poppins* provided a wealth of revenue for the Walt Disney Studios—and the funds that Walt needed to build New Orleans Square and Pirates of the Caribbean.

Pirates of the Caribbean was initially conceived as a standard wax museum, filled with pirate figures in staged settings. But working on four attractions for the New York World's Fair—including the development of the first human Audio-Animatronic (Abraham Lincoln) and an efficient way to move large groups of people through an experience (the use of boats in It's a Small World)—gave Walt and his designers the idea and the know-how to forego that notion and make Pirates of the Caribbean a fully animated, totally immersive environment.

When Pirates of the Caribbean opened in 1967, the fake skeletons available to the Disney designers were unconvincing and looked like tacky Halloween decorations, so real specimens, which had previously been used for research, were purchased from UCLA's Medical Center.

By request of the Anaheim Fire Department, Pirates of the Caribbean is equipped with a system that, in the event of an actual fire, automatically shuts down the authentic "burning town" effect found at the end of the ride, so that firefighters can pinpoint the real blaze and not waste time battling artificial flames.

Pirates of the Caribbean was the first attraction designed with so much happening simultaneously that it was impossible to see, hear, and experience everything in one pass. As a result, it revolutionized Disneyland, by guaranteeing what has become the holy grail of the amusement park industry: the return visit.

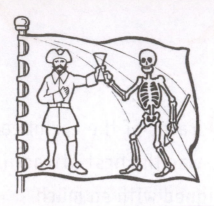

Most guests leave the park only having understood the first line ("Yo ho, yo ho, a pirate's life for me") of the Pirates of the Caribbean theme song. Although hard to decipher, the rest goes as follows: "We pillage, we plunder, we rifle, and loot/Drink up, me 'earties, yo ho/We kidnap and ravage and don't give a hoot/Drink up me 'earties, yo ho."

More Disneyland guests have ridden the Pirates of the Caribbean than any other attraction.

311 MILLION

park guests who have ridden the
Pirates of the Caribbean

20

unsavory acts mentioned in the
Pirates of the Caribbean theme song
"A Pirate's Life for Me;" they include
plundering, pillaging, rifling, looting,
kidnapping, ravaging, extorting,
pilfering, filching, sacking, marauding,
embezzling, hijacking, kindling,
charring, inflaming, igniting,
burning up the city, begging,
and drinking

Disneyland greeted its one-millionth guest after less than eight weeks of operation.

It was a combination of the letters he got from kids (who wanted to visit the place where Mickey Mouse lived), his frustration that no city park offered equipment that parents could (comfortably) ride along with their children, and his visit to The Henry Ford (a living history museum in Michigan) that fed Walt's plan to create a "land" where families could spend the day together.

The original site Walt had his eye on was the six-acre tract across from his studios in Burbank, California (currently the location of the hat-shaped Walt Disney Feature Animation Building), but as his team came up with more and more ideas, his Mickey Mouse Park evolved into Disneylandia (ultimately, just Disneyland), and the location shifted south to an orange grove in Anaheim, California.

naheim, which in the early 1950s was predicted to become the population center of Southern California, was selected from among more than seventy proposed sites for Disneyland. Beach towns were the most frequently suggested, but Walt believed it would be impossible for his park to compete against the ocean.

$10,000

price paid by the Fujishige family, in 1954, for the 56 acres of strawberry fields across from Disneyland

$99.9 MILLION

price paid by Disneyland, in the late 1990s, to the Fujishige family for 52.5 of the 56 acres

To raise money to build the park, Walt borrowed on his own life insurance policy, cashed in on property he owned, and got the American Broadcasting Company (then brand new) to contribute more than $500,000 in exchange for a one-third ownership and a television series. The Disney Company not only bought out ABC's interest two years later, but in 1995, they bought ABC.

Scentertainment refers to the enhancement of the Disneyland experience by incorporating smells into various park areas and attractions, be it the aroma of chocolate, caramel apple, and waffle cone outside the Candy Palace on Main Street or the musky odor that hits you as you descend into the Pirates of the Caribbean.

The pine trees, ocean salt, and orange groves that guests smell while Soarin' Over California are created when a pound of small translucent beads (each about the size of a peppercorn) is loaded into a cannon-like device called a Smellitzer, and air is shot through them, to release the scent. The Smellitzer also contains a micro-fan, which clears the air of the first scent in time to release the next one.

To prove that the innovative ride system proposed for Soarin' Over California would fly, designers built a working model, using an Erector Set and pink yarn.

Soarin' Over California is projected at forty-eight frames per second, which is double the speed of a normal motion picture. This results in a sharper, clearer image, with exceptional definition.

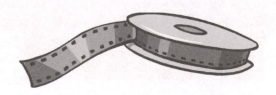

The best seat from which to watch Soarin' Over California is in the first row, which boards from Line 1 and will put you on the top tier when the attraction starts. This not only insures that you "fly" the highest, but that you have an unobstructed view without other guests' feet dangling in front of you.

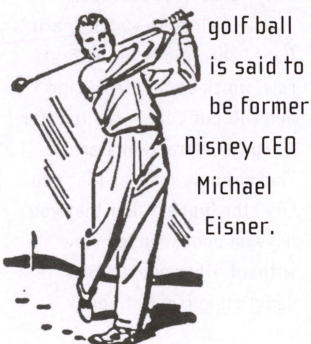

In Soarin' Over California, the man that can be seen hitting the golf ball is said to be former Disney CEO Michael Eisner.

4 MINUTES, 41 SECONDS

total travel time to go Soarin' Over California

150

pairs of sunglasses lost on a typical
summer day at Disneyland Resort

8

number of graveyards in Disneyland
(4 at the Haunted Mansion, 1 in Frontierland,
1 on Tom Sawyer Island, 1 along Storybook
Land Canal, and 1 in Finding Nemo
Submarine Voyage)

FAA regulations require that any building over 200 feet tall must have a red aviation light on top; because of that, the Tower of Terror (in California Adventure) was purposely built to be exactly 199 feet tall, as designers felt that a flashing beacon would destroy the illusion of a 1939 hotel.

In the first interior room of the Tower of Terror (the one with the TV set), there is a shelf lined with books that are initialed T.Z. at the top, and whose titles are those of popular episodes in the original *Twilight Zone* TV series.

According to the employee manuals from 1955 to 2000, male workers at Disneyland were not permitted to have facial hair. Which means that Walt Disney—who wore a moustache—would not have been allowed to work at his own park.

ABOUT THE AUTHOR

David Hoffman is a television writer, a frequent on-camera correspondent, and the author of over a dozen books about popular culture, for which, in recent years, he has been paid to play with toys, challenge untapped cooking skills (with the help of some big-name chefs), and eat and shop his way across the country. He lives in Los Angeles, where he likes to pretend this is hard work.

DISCLAIMER

This book is a fun, enjoyable tribute to "The Happiest Place on Earth" and is in no way authorized, endorsed, or sponsored by, nor is it affiliated with, the Disneyland Resort, the Walt Disney Company, or any of their subsidiaries, affiliates, or sponsors. All facts and figures were accurate, to the best of our knowledge, at press time. Disneyland, the Magic Kingdom, Mickey Mouse, Minnie Mouse, Donald Duck, Fantasyland, Storybookland, Tomorrowland, Adventureland, Frontierland, New Orleans Square, Toontown, the Mickey Mouse Club, Mouseketeers, Disneyland Band, Disney University, Disneyland Monorail, Disneyland Railroad, Primeval World, Fantasy in the Sky, Remember...Dreams Come True, Main Street Electrical Parade, Great Moments with Mr. Lincoln, Audio-Animatronics, Sleeping Beauty Castle, It's a Small World, Mad Tea Party, Peter Pan's Flight, King Arthur's Carousel, Submarine Voyage, Star Tours, Space Mountain, the Matterhorn, Innoventions, Adventure Thru Inner Space, Captain EO, Tarzan's Treehouse, Jungle Cruise, Enchanted Tiki Room, Indiana Jones Adventure, Tom Sawyer Island, Club 33, Pirates of the Caribbean, Haunted Mansion, Big Thunder Mountain Railroad, Splash Mountain, Soarin' Over California, Tower of Terror, California Adventure, and any other Disney character or Disneyland Resort ride, attraction, or locale that was mentioned in the book (but perhaps not mentioned on this page) are all registered trademarks and property of the Walt Disney Company, all rights reserved.

Whew.